PAY
YOURSELF
FIRST

A FINANCIAL GUIDE
FOR DOCTORS ENTERING PRACTICE

DAVID A. BURD, CFP®
JAMES S. HEMPHILL, CFP®, CIMA®, CPWA®

Second Edition

Text copyright © 2017
David A. Burd & James S. Hemphill

All Rights Reserved

Published By:
TGS Financial Advisors
170 N. Radnor Chester Rd.
Radnor, PA 19087

www.tgsfinancial.com

TABLE OF CONTENTS

Disclosure

As physicians understand only too well, we live in a world of litigation and regulation. For this reason, and to protect you as a reader, we offer the following legal caution.

David A. Burd, CFP® and James S. Hemphill, CFP® CIMA® CPWA® are Managing Directors of TGS Financial Advisors, an SEC registered investment advisor located in Radnor, Pennsylvania. They have written this book as an introduction to the financial challenges faced by physicians beginning practice.

The intent of this book is to help you to understand the financial landscape, not to give you a detailed roadmap to your own individual destination. No reader should regard this book as the receipt of, or a substitute for, personalized advice from Mr. Burd, Mr. Hemphill, or from TGS Financial Advisors, or from any other investment professional.

Please remember that different types of investments involve varying degrees of risk. Therefore, it should not be assumed that the future performance of any specific investment, investment product, or investment strategy (including the investments and/or investment strategies referenced in this book), or any of the book's non-investment related content, will be profitable, prove successful, or be applicable to any individual's specific situation.

Should a reader have any questions about how to apply the principles in this book to his or her individual situation, the reader is encouraged to consult with the professional advisors of his or her choosing.

Foreword

> *"Annual income twenty pounds, annual expenditure nineteen pounds nineteen shillings and six pence, result happiness. Annual income twenty pounds, annual expenditure twenty pounds ought and six, result misery."*
>
> Charles Dickens, *David Copperfield*

If only it were as simple as Charles Dickens wrote in 1850! Well, maybe it is.

As a teacher and mentor in a Family Medicine Residency Program for close to 25 years, I have been amazed that residents and medical students have so little working knowledge of personal finance and financial planning. One reason for this lack of knowledge may be that we find the subject overwhelming. Many of us graduate medical school with such a large debt burden that financial security may seem like a distant pipe dream. We may also feel that, as intelligent, educated people, we should already know these things. We feel embarrassed to ask financial questions that we fear are too rudimentary.

Some of us were lucky enough to grow up in homes where financial matters were routinely discussed, but I suspect that most of us did not. This is unfortunate. Something has been lost by no longer talking across the dinner table about finances, sharing stories about grandparents who used "Christmas clubs" to save for holiday presents, or who saved up for years to pay cash for a new car. The availability of easy credit has helped to form a younger generation who have never lived the reality of financial discipline, deferred gratification, and saving up for something *before* buying it!

I think this book is a great way for young physicians to take a big first step toward personal financial literacy. It teaches important financial lessons in a lucid, simple manner. It also challenges some common approaches espoused by "financial planners" who may have conflicts of interest. It is an easy, focused read. If our significant others read it as well, it could be a catalyst for important family conversations about what it should really mean to "be rich."

If we can learn to "pay ourselves first," then perhaps we can help our children pursue their own educational dreams, retire at a reasonable age and live comfortably after working so hard for so long. This book is a good start.

John Russell, M.D.
2016

Introduction

"If I was doing this job to make money, I would not be doing this job."

Neonatologist, Pacific Northwest

"The only way not to think about money is to have a great deal of it."

Edith Wharton

Some years back I was on the board of a local non-profit. I was brought in to help solve the school's perpetual financial crisis. Over several years, we put financial controls in place, recruited more committed and generous board members, secured new sources of support, and began a systematic fundraising program.

During those rebuilding years, most of our conversation on the board was about money, not mission. We had no ability to improve programs because all of our energy was consumed with finding enough dollars to keep the doors open.

One of my takeaways from this experience was that being short of money can dominate your thought, in a way that interferes with matters of much greater meaning.

I don't know any physicians who chose their careers for strictly monetary reasons. Many knew they wanted to be doctors before their understanding of finances went beyond how many comic books they could buy with a week's allowance.

The greatest rewards of being a physician, according to the physicians we know, are those arising from the practice of medicine itself—the chance to work with capable peers, to save lives and improve their quality, to create profound value in the world.

The worst aspect of contemporary medicine, according to pretty much every physician we know, is the endless paperwork and time concerned with who gets paid, how much and when, by which third-party, for doing what to whom. (Electronic medical records come a close second.)

I'm entirely persuaded by the idea that money must be secondary to a physician's mission. Yet as a financial advisor with doctors as clients and as friends, I'm also very much aware of two things:

> Doctors as a group significantly underperform most other professions at accumulating wealth, in relation to their incomes.

> Many doctors worry, chronically and seriously, about their own personal money situations.

This book is intended to provide some guidance about how to deal with money issues, systematically and sensibly, from the very beginning of your career, so that money can occupy its proper place in your life—as background noise that does not distract from the real sources of joy, satisfaction and contribution—your career, family, friends and patients.

Jim Hemphill
Radnor, PA
Summer 2013

After years of schooling and punishing workdays of twelve or more hours during residency and fellowship, you are ready to start your career as a physician. You will finally begin to reap the financial rewards you deserve for all of your hard work.

Chapter 1: You've Made It

As a new physician, you have deferred gratification like few other professionals on earth. You have excelled in every academic environment, graduating at the top of your class from high school and college, secured admission to medical school, graduated from medical school, and then worked insane hours as a resident and perhaps a fellow for ridiculously low wages.

No other professional occupation requires a similar length of training. Any medical degree generally requires twenty years in classrooms, followed by at least four years in residency. Add in a fellowship, and it is entirely plausible that a new attending physician will have invested more than 30,000 hours in classwork and hands-on training. (A thoracic surgeon may spend almost 50,000 hours in education and training, not including non-class study hours.)

If you were paid $50,000 a year as a resident or fellow, working 80 hours per week, you earned as little as $12.50 per hour—less than the waiter at the local tavern on a busy Friday night. Plus, a typical doctor has accumulated more than $185,000 in school loans.[1]

You are now in a position, for the first time, where your hard work will start being fairly rewarded. In the Mid-Atlantic states, where our financial advisory practice is located, a new hospitalist might see his income increase from $50,000 to $175,000, and a cardiac surgeon might earn a starting salary of $300,000 or more.[2]

You need to make sure that your increased income will provide the

---

[1] American Association of Medical Colleges, *Medical Student Education: Debt, Costs and Loan Repayment Fact Card 2016.*

[2] Since physician incomes can vary dramatically by specialty, please understand a crucial fact right away—*it is not your top line income that will determine your ultimate financial security*. It is the choices you make about what you *do* with your income—the relative allocation to savings versus consumption, that will determine your financial outcomes. In practice, it may actually be easier for a pediatrician to build real wealth, properly defined, than a neurosurgeon.

maximum benefit, for you and your family, over your entire lifetime.

Reading this book should take you less than one hour. We hope it benefits you for decades to come.

Within one year of beginning practice as a physician, you will make the key choices that will either place you on a path toward financial independence, or establish a high-consumption lifestyle you may be unable to sustain years from now, as you begin to make the transition from work into retirement.

Chapter 2: Inflection Point

> *"There is a tide in the affairs of men, which taken at the flood, leads on to fortune. Omitted, all the voyage of their life is bound in shallows and in miseries.*

> William Shakespeare, *Julius Caesar*

Your lifetime financial outcomes will depend on a host of choices, large and small, that you will make over decades. But each of those choices will not carry equal weight. The decisions you make at a limited number of inflection points will largely determine the financial arc of your entire life.

For most physicians, the single most important period lies at the transition from residency or fellowship to practice as an attending physician. Just as there is a "golden window" in emergency medical treatment, so is there a crucial period in your financial life, within the first three years of starting practice.

Of course, the choices you are about to make are only the latest in a lifelong series, each of which has altered the trajectory of your life:

> ➤ The first time you thought, "I want to be a doctor when I grow up."

> ➤ The point when you decided to take more challenging high school courses in order to get into a better college.

> ➤ When you declared your college major, perhaps choosing biology or another hard science, and submitting to the rigors and competition of the pre-med curriculum.

> ➤ Your choice to defer your first big payday (again) by pursuing and accepting a challenging fellowship.

Each of these decisions is best understood not as an *event*, but as the beginning of a *process*. Each choice was followed by commitment, action, event and consequence.

Now all of those choices have borne fruit. Your income has increased sharply, and your new challenge is deciding how to allocate that increased income. The default choice, for physicians as for American society as a whole, leans heavily toward immediate consumption. The alternative choice balances consumption today against financial independence tomorrow. Choosing financial independence creates challenges both economic and psychological, which we'll explore more fully in the coming pages.

Don't be discouraged, either by the fact of your debt load or by the knowledge that others are ahead of you financially. The moving parts of accumulating wealth are actually well understood, and there are known habits and strategies that constitute best practice. In the following chapters we'll outline how you can take your first steps along a path toward achieving walkaway wealth by the time you are sixty years old.

Regardless of the financial choices you make in the coming weeks and months, you will do challenging and valuable work, with peers who are among the most capable individuals on the planet. You will bring healing and comfort to your fellow humans, saving lives and improving health.

All of this is good. *Don't ignore the power of choice at the inflection point.*

The two narratives in this chapter are altered as to name, location and specialty, and families have been combined into composites, in order to carefully protect client confidentiality. What we haven't changed are the numbers. These are not hypotheticals or projections. They are the real results of real doctors.

Chapter 3: A Tale of Two Doctors

Marie and Edward were both anesthesiologists. They met at a medical conference and married in their thirties. They bought a charming home, built in the 1920s but recently remodeled, in an upscale suburb of Philadelphia, within easy commuting distance of the two hospitals where they worked.

Marie was a partner in an independent practice, while Ed was an employee of a large urban hospital. As anesthesiologists, both earned high incomes, though not as high as those of some surgical sub-specialties. From early in their careers, each contributed the maximum allowed to their retirement plans at work. Marie's partnership made the maximum employer contribution to her plan as well, and she saved at least another 10% of her income to after-tax accounts. Both invested primarily in common stocks.

Their two children went to public schools in their highly-rated school district. They bought a cottage on a lake in the mountains. They vacationed mostly at their cottage, though they took an occasional trip to Europe or Disney World.

Marie worked with a financial advisor from the beginning of her career. Ed managed his funds himself until they began to consider early retirement, then began to work with the same advisor.

At age 58, with the younger child in college, Ed went to half-time work. They bought a three-story row house in the historic Society Hill section of Philadelphia, which they gutted and rebuilt, with Ed supervising construction. They installed an elevator, a wine cellar, and enough bookshelves for Marie's thousands of books.

At Marie's age 58, Ed's age 61, with both kids finished college, they walked away, retiring from medical practice, selling their house in the suburbs and moving into the city, near the music and culture they loved. Their net worth was over $8 million. They looked forward to decades of active retirement, without a hint of financial worry.

John was an orthopedist, and his wife Anne an attorney with her own practice. Based on John's high income, they bought a historically-significant mansion on Philadelphia's Main Line, where they raised three children, all of whom went to exclusive and expensive private schools.

Starting in the 1980s, John saved the maximum pre-tax salary deferral to his 401k, but he and his partners could never agree about whether they wished to cover employees in their retirement plan, and his practice did not make any employer contributions.

They regarded Anne's income as their vacation money, and did not save much of it. Anne did not set up any employer-based retirement plan, though she did make occasional contributions to an Individual Retirement Account. John managed their investments, and he lost significant funds when the tech bubble collapsed in the early 2000s.

In his late 50s, John experienced health problems and had to retire from his orthopedic practice. He transitioned into medical administration, at a much reduced salary. At the same time, Anne's legal practice began to wind down.

When both were age 62, they were referred to our advisory practice by a friend, another physician client. When we met them, their total investment net worth (excluding real estate but including all retirement assets) was less than $400,000.

We did a full financial proposal for them, targeting retirement at age 70 with an income level that would replace John's after-tax salary, an amount in the low six figures. Since all of their kids were grown and out of the house, we recommended they sell their big house and downsize to a condo. The net proceeds from the change of residence would have been over $500,000, to be added to their investment portfolio. We projected the annual savings on upkeep would be in excess of $40,000. Over the eight years until age 70, we hoped to help them build their portfolio to more than $1.5 million.

They never sold the big house, because they wanted plenty of bedrooms for when their grandchildren came to visit. John continued to make the maximum annual contribution to his 401k each year, but Anne began to draw down her IRA to pay for several weddings. Seven years later, their investment net worth had grown to just over $600,000.

John has now retired, and Anne has closed down her legal practice. Their investments will provide retirement cash flow to supplement their Social Security, with total annual income under $100,000. They hope their investment assets will last for at least ten years, at which time they will finally sell their house and downsize.

Their situation is a far cry from poverty. They have more assets, and will spend more income in retirement, than the majority of Americans. But this is surely not what they expected their retirement to look like, back in the 1990s at the peak of John's career, when their annual income was over half a million dollars.

The pattern of your life will be your own, but you are likely to find echoes of the lifestyle choices made by these two physician families, and of their financial consequences, in your own experience.

One factor in particular is worth noting—it is not your gross level of income that will buy you financial security, it is the decisions you make on how to allocate that income stream—the relative percentages directed toward consumption and toward savings.

As a physician, you are going to be rich no matter what—by somebody's definition. You need to be sure that the definition of wealth you choose is the one that gets you the results you want, both here at the beginning of your career, and decades from now at the end.

Chapter 4: What is Wealth?

> *"Two roads diverged in a wood and I –*
> *I took the one less-traveled by,*
> *And that has made all the difference."*

Robert Frost, *The Road Not Taken*

Your challenges are born of your own earned success and achievement. Your choices require deciding how to allocate a relative abundance of income and opportunity. The path you follow will depend on the definition of wealth that you choose. So let's ask two related, difficult questions:

➢ *What is wealth?*

➢ *Who is rich?*

When many Americans think of wealth, they picture Donald Trump, with his television show, bad hair, serial wives and multiple residences. In Trump's world, wealth is measured by the visibility of the material objects you display, by your own notoriety, and by the control you can exercise over other people.[3]

In reality, there have been times when Trump has had negative net worth—he has actually *owed* more on his various projects and properties than he *owned*. But he never moved out of the mansion with the gold-plated bathroom fixtures, or stopped getting his $200 bad haircuts.

If you want to be financially independent, you're going to need a better concept of wealth. Here's our working definition: You are rich when you can maintain the lifestyle you choose, for as long as you live, without ever being required to work.

---

[3] The first edition of this book was written when Mr. Trump's Presidential ambitions were an unlikely rumor. We've retained the example as an object lesson about how many Americans react to the *display* of apparent wealth and success, rather than the *reality* of prudent investment practice and the financial independence that results.

There are two key components of this definition:

➢ You define your target lifestyle. The cost of that *chosen* lifestyle determines the capital needed to sustain it indefinitely.

➢ You will be targeting walkaway wealth, but you will not be *required* to actually walk away once you attain it.[4]

Let's look more closely at this relationship between lifestyle and capital:

➢ A cardiac surgeon who chooses a lifestyle featuring a mansion in a posh suburb, a beachfront home at the shore, a new Mercedes every three years for each spouse, and annual European villa vacations with the extended family, might need an investment portfolio worth $20 million to be "rich" by our functional definition, which is based on the ability to produce cash flow.

➢ A public schoolteacher whose defined lifestyle includes a modest house in a good school district, who drives the same car for 200,000 miles and vacations in a tent at a National Park, who can expect a taxpayer-funded public pension and lifetime medical benefits, might be functionally rich with less than $500,000 of investment assets.

How can the person with much less income and lower net worth be functionally richer? *Because she can walk away and keep it all going.*

The table below shows the income-replacement ratio for the

---

[4] Nobody is going to walk up to you and say, "We've just learned you are financially independent. Put down that stethoscope and slowly walk away." Consider Warren Buffett, in his 80s, worth $55 billion and still going to work at Berkshire Hathaway every day.

schoolteacher and the surgeon:

	Teacher	Physician
Working:		
Income	$70,000	$350,000
Marginal tax bracket	15%	33%
At retirement:		
Retirement savings	$250,000	$1,000,000
Pension	$35,000	$0
Social Security	$24,200	$30,000
Total scheduled income	$59,200	$30,000
Income replacement ratio	*84%*	*8%*

With some minor changes, that public school teacher's fact pattern could also apply to a pediatrician, hospitalist, or family medicine physician. This illustrates one of the paradoxes of physician wealth. It is impossible for a family medicine doc to duplicate the present lifestyle of the typical cardiac surgeon, yet it is similarly difficult for that surgeon to accumulate enough wealth to preserve his income in retirement. To build walkaway wealth, the surgeon must save millions of dollars to taxable accounts, after paying taxes on earned income that can approach or even exceed 50%, once state and local taxes are added in.

Your chosen lifestyle will probably fall between these extremes. Still, you should be highly intentional about that lifestyle, because it is your choice of lifestyle that will determine the target wealth needed to sustain it indefinitely.

Next, let's examine the idea of walkaway wealth. Keep in mind that attaining true financial independence does not require you to stop working—but it does give you the option. We often hear from younger doctors: "I don't need to be financially independent at age 60, because I plan to keep working into my 70s."

Maybe yes, and maybe no.

Historically, physicians were among the least likely professionals to seek early retirement. Who would want to leave the prestigious, intellectually challenging, and psychologically rewarding job of healer? As recently as the late 1980s, the average physician did not retire until after age 70. Yet a 2012 survey by the Physicians Foundation found that over 60% of doctors would retire *immediately* if they had the financial means, an increase of one-third in only four years.

Based on more than a quarter-century of working with doctors, we suspect the chance you will wish to retire early is greater than you think now, at the beginning of your career. The career choices of physicians have changed as medicine has become more bureaucratized, as paperwork increases even as clinical autonomy decreases, as reimbursements decline while treatment expectations rise, and as the amount of uncompensated medical care continues to increase.

We hope your medical practice will be so rewarding that you will choose to practice into your 70s, even if you have the wealth to walk away at 60. We certainly understand that our nation faces a looming shortage of physicians. But just in case medical practice becomes even more stressful, we like the idea you might be able to regard your work as a free choice, and not as a perpetual, involuntary economic necessity.

Doctors have a unique disadvantage in building wealth, because they are expected to exhibit a high-status lifestyle. Compared to other highly-compensated professionals, doctors are less likely to achieve financial independence. Here at the inflection point, as you begin your career, you have the best opportunity of your life to increase your comfort and status, while still putting away much greater savings.

Chapter 5: The Trap of Status

"It is neither wealth nor splendor; but tranquility and occupation which give you happiness."

Thomas Jefferson

Nobody expects a plumber to drive a BMW and live in a big house. That doesn't mean there are no successful plumbers. Far from it. And surely there are wealthy plumbers happily driving Bimmers and living large. But nobody *expects* it of them.

On the other hand, everyone has expectations of doctors—how they look, act, and dress, what they drive, where they live. Those expectations are powerful.

In evaluating our status, we compare ourselves to a peer group. Psychologists call this process *social comparison*. Human beings are primates, not rodents; we are chimpanzees more than squirrels. We are social, competitive, and status-oriented. We're hard-wired to keep up with the Joneses, much more than we are to save our acorns for the winter. It would be difficult to overstate the power of the psychological imperative to achieve higher status.

In the United States, the dominant status hierarchy is socio-economic—how much you make, what you spend, and what you own. The default choice for most young doctors is to spend now and save later, a sequence that provides both material comfort and psychological reinforcement.

At first, greater income and higher spending are associated with greater happiness. But that gain in happiness is likely to be temporary. As people adapt to a new, higher level of status, they begin to compare themselves to a similarly successful peer group, and the psychic benefit of their elevated status erodes. The law of diminishing returns surely applies. Raising your income from $25,000 to $50,000 has way more psychic benefit than the identical dollar increase from $300,000 to $325,000.

Spending on possessions has the most transient effect on happiness, while spending on relationships and experiences has more durable emotional benefits. Unlike status based on earning or spending, research suggests that attaining $1 million of net worth is associated with a permanent increase in confidence and self-esteem.

Society's expectations drive spending behaviors that stand in direct conflict to the savings habits needed to build financial independence. Every dollar spent is a dollar that cannot be saved, and vice versa.

But isn't this really a question about the *timing* of savings? Why not spend your available cash flow now, getting your household established and making up for lost time, and get around to saving later, cutting back on your future spending as needed?

Unfortunately, the relationship of wealth to happiness is asymmetric. Moving up is often only temporarily rewarding. But losing ground—suffering even a limited reduction in socio-economic status—is durably painful.

Just as the "spend now" strategy fulfills status expectations, the "save later" aspect will violate them, since it will eventually require a painful reduction in displayed wealth, comfort and status. Ignore the purely practical sacrifices—at the peak of your career, do you really think you will fancy trading in your Lexus for a Toyota Camry? The psychic cost of reducing spending sharply, in order to catch up on retirement savings, would be profound.

Far better to retain a healthy baseline skepticism about status from the beginning. After all, you're not required to meet anyone else's expectation of how you live. Not your mother's, your colleagues', society's, nor those of your Mercedes Benz salesman, real estate broker or financial advisor.

Our culture's dominant status hierarchy is socio-economic, but it isn't the only available metric for keeping score. As a physician you can—and should—focus your status self-evaluation on an entirely different hierarchy, that of reputation. Reputational status is about respect and trust. And in this hierarchy, physicians have few equals.

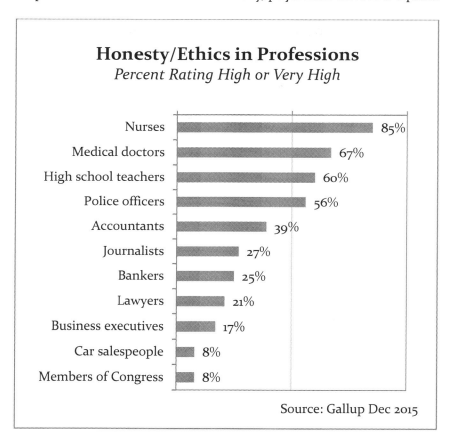

Honesty/Ethics in Professions
Percent Rating High or Very High

Profession	Percent
Nurses	85%
Medical doctors	67%
High school teachers	60%
Police officers	56%
Accountants	39%
Journalists	27%
Bankers	25%
Lawyers	21%
Business executives	17%
Car salespeople	8%
Members of Congress	8%

Source: Gallup Dec 2015

In a society suffering from a crisis of distrust in institutions and professions, Americans still trust their doctors.

Given that even the most successful physician may be unable to keep pace with the spending of a hedge fund manager, Hollywood mogul, or reality TV star, and that Americans already trust and respect you much more than any of those other persons, why not opt out of the consumption competition entirely? Let someone else own that BMW 7-series, and the debts and worries that go with it. *Choosing to build your self-evaluation around your profession can be a powerful tool to push back against the consumption imperative.*

Remember, the highest status activity you engage in, and the highest value you contribute to the world, will always be simply your work as a physician.

In the United States, the typical income of a new attending physician is $175,000 or more, in the top 5% of earnings for all American workers. Yet here at the beginning of your career, your assets are probably smaller than those owned by the average public school teacher. Asset poor and cash flow rich—in your first years of practice, everyone will want a piece of that cash flow.

Chapter 6: You Want a Piece of Me?

"Everyone wants to get a piece of me."

Tiger Woods

As a new attending physician starting practice, you will have the largest amount of uncommitted cash flow you've ever enjoyed. With lots of disposable income and a pristine credit history, banks will be eager to loan you money. Real estate agents will compete to show you houses. Car dealers will offer you top-tier lease terms on new cars.

We are a consumer-driven society. A clean, bright, well-lighted house in beautiful surroundings can be a lasting joy. A well-made luxury automobile appeals on many levels. Dinner at a fine restaurant with someone you love is one of life's great pleasures. With all of these positive goods, it is difficult to draw a bright line that says, "This is enough."

Yet just as income and status are subject to the law of diminishing returns, so are consumer goods. A new Toyota Camry is a nicer vehicle than a used Honda Civic, and a Mercedes nicer still. But the extra functionality you buy for the next $10,000 at the margin becomes ever smaller as the absolute price increases.

The same principle of diminishing utility per dollar of marginal expenditure applies even more powerfully to houses. There is even a name for that first, too-large and too-expensive home—they call it "the doctor house." As we'll explain more fully in Chapter 13, no other purchase decision has as much potential to permanently disrupt your progress toward financial freedom as buying too much house.

Let's touch on another purchase decision most new doctors make: the choice about how much life insurance coverage to buy, and what type. Consider a specific not-so-hypothetical. Assume that in your first three months of work you've saved $20,000. What should you do with it?

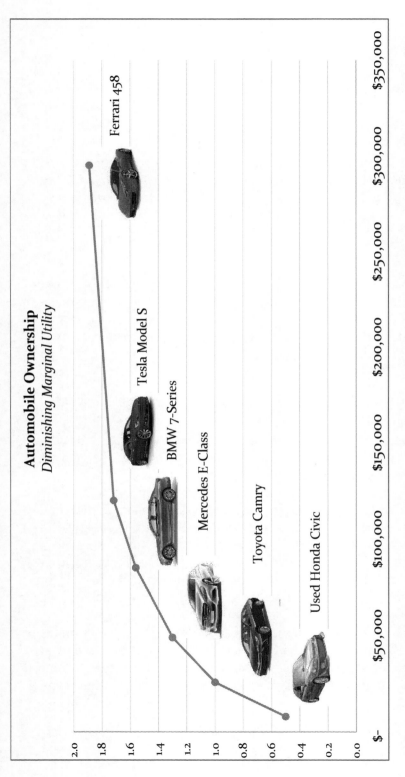

Automobile Ownership
Diminishing Marginal Utility

Ferrari 458

Tesla Model S

BMW 7-Series

Mercedes E-Class

Toyota Camry

Used Honda Civic

2.0
1.8
1.6
1.4
1.2
1.0
0.8
0.6
0.4
0.2
0.0

$- $50,000 $100,000 $150,000 $200,000 $250,000 $300,000 $350,000

A more expensive car is a nicer car, but the degree of additional style and function diminishes as the cost increases. What exactly does the utility function on the *y*-axis measure? A variety of things, some objective and quantifiable, and some subjective and impossible to value. (How much is that new car smell worth? How about the prancing horse emblem on the Ferrari?) The impossibility of precisely quantifying the worth of higher-status goods is real, and a key driver of the trap of status.

- If you buy a $500,000 face whole life insurance policy with a first-year premium of $20,000, the insurance agent will earn a commission of $8,000 or more. [5]

- On the other hand, you could buy a $2 million twenty-year level-premium term life insurance contract for $1,100 per year, and invest almost $20,000 with an investment advisor. At a 1.5% annual advisory fee, the investment guy will earn $300 managing your portfolio over the first year. (Actually, he will lose money. That $300 will not cover the personnel costs involved in simply opening accounts and processing paperwork.)

- Perhaps best of all, you could buy the term insurance and use the remainder of the $20,000 to pay down your education loans, earning a risk-free after-tax return of 6.8%.

Who has the greater incentive to chase after your business? Obviously, it's the insurance guy soliciting purchase of the whole life insurance policy. Yet the fact that the insurance salesman has the greater financial incentive to pursue your business does *not* mean the decision to own whole life insurance, potentially at the expense of retirement saving or debt reduction, is optimal for you and your family.

Don't get us wrong. We believe most doctors should put insurance protections in place *before* they begin building an investment portfolio. Protecting your earnings with disability insurance, your family with life insurance, your assets with liability insurance, and your career with malpractice insurance, are all foundations of your lifetime financial security. When we begin work with a new

---

[5] We've been accused of being "anti-insurance." That really isn't the case. Both of this book's authors pay large annual premiums for insurance coverage, including term life, disability, professional liability, and so on. Suffice it to say that the arguments in favor of *whole life insurance* (also called *cash value insurance* or *permanent life insurance*) as a long-term investment are complex, and we are not proponents of its purchase by early-career professionals.

physician client, one of the first things we do is make a referral to the right insurance agent—one who will make sure you own the appropriate insurance for your circumstances and career stage.[6]

Plenty of other people are going to get well-paid based on the decisions you make. Amid the excitement of all the new opportunities, and the distraction of competing sales presentations, try to keep one principle in mind: *Pay yourself first*.

---

[6] As fee-only financial advisors, we do not sell any type of insurance, or any other commission-based financial product.

Whatever your cash flow, it will be easy to find opportunities to spend it. That is why you need to make savings your first priority, not your last. Of all of the components of a successful wealth-building program, none is more important than time.

> *"Work expands to fill the time allotted to its completion."*
>
> *Parkinson's Law*

Spending, like work, can easily expand to consume most or all of your after-tax income. Many doctors choose to acquire the house, the cars, the vacation home, and the rest of the lifestyle elements first, assuming they can take care of the savings later. Unfortunately, this sequence is problematic, for two reasons. As we've discussed, the first is the psychology of status; it is easy to move up, desperately unpleasant to move down.

The second is the magic—and tyranny—of compound interest. Consider two saving/spending sequences:

> ➤ Save 20% of your income starting at age 35, and continue through age 45, then stop. (Ten years of savings.)

> ➤ Spend your income when you begin practice at age 35, then start saving aggressively at age 45, putting away 20% of income, and continue through retirement at age 65. (Twenty years of savings.)

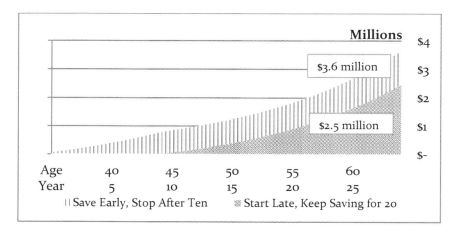

Here's the same data set in table form:[7]

	Save Early, Stop After Ten	Start Late, Keep Saving for 20
Total Savings	$500,000	$1,000,000
Total Earnings	$3,146,147	$1,471,146
Ending Value	$3,646,147	$2,471,146
Savings % of Total	13.7%	40.5%
Earnings % of Total	86.3%	59.5%

As you can see, the late saver does not ever catch up to the early saver, despite saving for twice as long and putting aside twice as many dollars out of income. *Almost 90% of the early saver's total wealth comes from earnings—from the compounding effect of money-making-money—while less than 60% of the late saver's wealth comes from compounding.*

This is a hidden cost to medical training that most non-physicians simply cannot understand. Not only have you studied longer than any other professional, incurred hundreds of thousands of dollars in education loans, and deferred a serious payday until your late 20s or even well into your 30s, you have also lost precious years of potential compounding on your savings.

We are *not* suggesting that you save for only ten years, and we are certainly not promising 8% annual returns. In fact, we expect long-term investment returns will be lower than normal over the next decade. But that means it is *more* important, not less, that you save significant amounts as soon as you can.

If you wait to start saving until you have acquired all of the things you want, you will lose precious compounding time you cannot

---

[7] In both the graph and the table, we are assuming gross income of $250,000, savings of $50,000 per year, investment returns of 8% per year, and ignoring both inflation and potential tax effects.

make up later.

Of course, there is no requirement to stop saving after ten years, and we don't recommend that anyone do so. If our early saver kept saving to age 65, she would accumulate over $6 million of investment net worth.

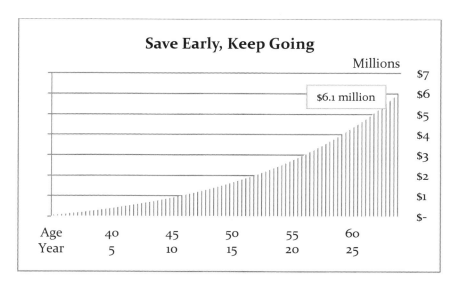

In the last chapter, we discussed the difficulty of drawing a bright line at the ideal "enough stuff" level. That is why you need to draw the line from the other direction. *Start off by determining the savings rate you will need to reach your financial independence goal, and then put structures in place to make those savings happen, as reliably and automatically as possible.* (More on this later.)

A great advantage of the automated-savings approach is that it makes spending choices much clearer. With savings fully funded before you see a single dollar in your spending account, you can spend as much as you like of your remaining after-tax cash flow in any way you choose, with a clear conscience and no misgivings.

Nobody expects you to drive a used Honda Civic and live in a rental apartment for the rest of your life. You can expect to live in a comfortable home, drive a safe car, enjoy meals out and relaxing vacations. Will that car be a Toyota Camry, an Acura MDX or a 7-Series BMW? Will your home be a 3,000 square foot used house in a great school district, or a 6,000 square foot new-construction McMansion? Will vacation be a week at the beach, or ten days skiing in Gstaad, Switzerland?

As financial advisors, we hate being in the position of saying, "Thou shalt not." Please understand that we are not making a moral judgment about which path you choose. Frankly, we believe you should buy what you darn well please. After all, you are the one who just finished long years of 11-hour workdays that would have brought us to our knees in a week. And the 7-series BMW is one terrific automobile. You could drive us to California sitting in that back seat and we wouldn't mind.

But understand that, in weighing these choices, you are not negotiating with us. You are negotiating with yourself—your future self, in ten, twenty, even thirty years from now. The choices you make will determine the balance between the lifestyle that you enjoy today, and the lifestyle and the stress levels that you'll experience in your 50s, 60s, even in your 70s and beyond.

Which will you choose?

> I will have the most beautiful home, and the hottest car, of anyone I knew in college.

> I will attain walkaway wealth before any of my medical school peers.

In twenty-five years, you can be the first of your peers with walkaway wealth. Or you can be age 60, living in a beautiful house, driving a luxury car, and worried that if you stop working you will run out of money within five years.

When we present to young doctors at hospitals, or meet with new attending physicians at our offices, the primary concern is almost always the same—*what should I do about my student loans?* Each year, new physicians start practice with larger loan balances. The choices to be made around loans are complex. Let's begin to make some sense of it all.

Chapter 8: Managing Your Student Loans

"He is rich enough who owes nothing."

French proverb

In 2015, the typical new attending physician began practice with over $185,000 in student loans. For graduates of public medical schools, the numbers were slightly lower. For graduates of private medical schools, slightly higher.[8]

This is a forbidding number, and many physicians have loan balances higher still. If you have borrowed to fund your medical education, you are likely to begin practice with *negative* net worth—beginning to build wealth not from nothing, but from less than zero.

Student loans are a serious challenge, but they need not be a permanent barrier to financial security. In this chapter, we'll share some basic facts about the student loan landscape and discuss features unique to federal loans. In the following chapter, we will put your loans into context, and present a strategy to optimize your savings, investing, and debt-paydown sequence.

There are two unique aspects of federal student loans that are vital for you to understand:

1) **Loan forgiveness.** Based on who you work for, and/or how long it takes to pay them back, you may be able to have a portion of your loan balances forgiven, possibly tax-free.

2) **Income-driven repayment options.** You may be able to reduce your monthly payments, stretch out your repayment period, and possibly qualify for loan forgiveness without public service.

---

[8] American Association of Medical Colleges, *Medical Student Education: Debt, Costs and Loan Repayment Fact Card 2016.*

Please note that both of these features apply *only* to federal student loans, such as Stafford loans, FFEL, Perkins loans, Grad Plus loans, and so on.

Let's examine two important ways you might be able to achieve forgiveness of a portion of your federal student loans:[9]

> ➤ **Work for a qualifying non-profit entity for 120 months while your loans are in repayment.** This is known as Public Sector Loan Forgiveness (PSLF). If you qualify for PSLF, the principal amount forgiven after ten years is tax-free. The remaining loan balance simply goes away, and there is no tax effect. This program was first made available to borrowers in 2007, and the first loans forgiven will be in 2017.

> ➤ **Elect an income-driven repayment option (IDR) that stretches out your loan payments over a period longer than the standard ten-year repayment schedule.** Any principal remaining after 20 or 25 years, depending on the repayment method chosen, may be forgiven. In this case, the principal amount is taxable income in the year it is forgiven.

If you can qualify, Public Service Loan Forgiveness is an extraordinary benefit. Here are some tips to keep in mind as you consider the possibility of Public Service Loan Forgiveness:

> ➤ Qualifying for PSLF forgiveness is measured in *months*, not in *dollars*.

> ➤ You accrue months toward PSLF only when working

---

[9] There are many ways to complete your medical education without taking out loans, from military service to practice in underserved communities— far too many to cover in this book, and far too few to allow most young physicians to begin practice without loans.

for a qualifying non-profit while your loans are in repayment. (About two-thirds of hospitals are non-profits.)

➤ Making monthly payments during residency and fellowship, even in relatively small amounts, accumulates months.

➤ You need to be very careful to pay your loans on a timely basis, and to file the necessary supporting paperwork each year, and at the end of the 120 months.[10]

The standard repayment schedule for all federal loans is ten years. Obviously, if all of your loans are already paid off by the end of the ten years required to qualify for Public Service Loan Forgiveness, you will get no financial benefit from PSLF. How can you pay over a longer period in order to benefit from loan forgiveness?

You will need to take advantage of one of the federal government's Income-Driven Repayment (IDR) plans. We'll use the example of the Revised Pay As You Earn program (REPAYE), first made available to federal borrowers in 2015.

➤ Take your gross income, and deduct 150% of the federal poverty line for your family size. This amount is considered your *discretionary income*,

➤ Under REPAYE you can reduce your payments to 10% of this discretionary income amount. You must re-calculate and refile each year.

➤ REPAYE allows you to reduce your monthly payments

---

[10] Many residents have asked about whether PSLF may change in future. For example, one recent proposal would have capped the maximum forgiveness at $57,500, though this would not apply to existing borrowers. How should you deal with this uncertainty? As advisors, our general principle is to plan to maximize opportunities under current law, while recognizing that any public sector benefit is subject to change.

dramatically while you are working during residency and fellowship, and still accumulate months toward the 120 required for Public Service Loan Forgiveness.

Here's a hypothetical that demonstrates the potential power of PSLF:

➢ Graduate from med school with $185,000 of Grad Plus loans at 6.8%.

➢ Spend your four years of residency in a non-profit hospital earning $50,000 per year. With discretionary income of just over $32,000 per year, as defined by REPAYE, you will pay only $268 per month. After four years, your loan principal will have grown to almost $228,000.

➢ Four years of fellowship in a non-profit hospital earning $60,000 per year, paying $352 per month on your loans, and ending with almost $280,000 of loan principal.

➢ Begin your career with two years of practice as an attending physician in a non-profit hospital earning $250,000 per year, while paying $1,935 per month. (It is only at this point that your payments are actually large enough to begin to reduce the principal.)

➢ At the end of two years as an attending, and ten years overall, the remaining $270,000 is forgiven tax-free.

➢ With your loans paid off, you can now work wherever you want, in either a for-profit or non-profit setting. [11]

---

[11] One of our young physician clients will complete his training in cardio-thoracic surgery at age 37, after medical school, residency, and five years of increasingly specialized fellowship. Wisely, he made income-driven repayments on his loans from the beginning of his residency. When he begins practice, he will need only one year of work at a non-profit hospital to have over $275,000 of student loans forgiven tax-free, even as he begins earning an income in the high six figures.

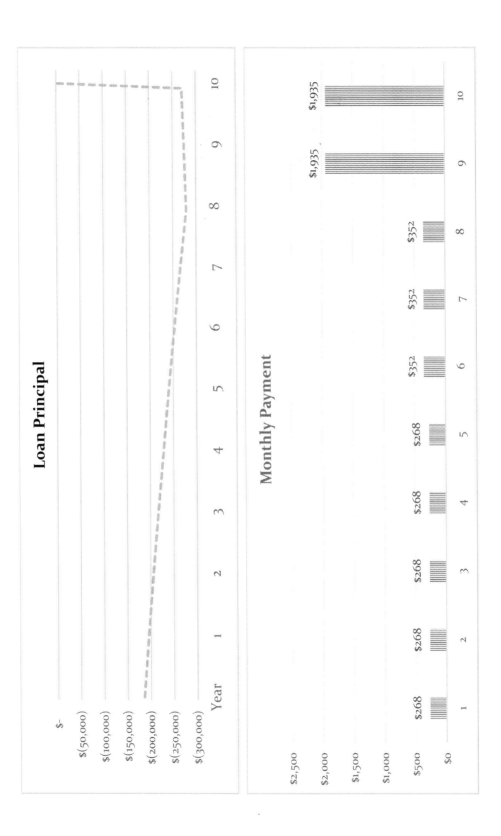

Loan Principal

$-
$(50,000)
$(100,000)
$(150,000)
$(200,000)
$(250,000)
$(300,000)

Year   1   2   3   4   5   6   7   8   9   10

Monthly Payment

$2,500
$2,000
$1,500
$1,000
$500
$0

$268 $268 $268 $268 $268 $352 $352 $352 $1,935 $1,935

1   2   3   4   5   6   7   8   9   10

What if you don't expect to accumulate 120 months in a non-profit setting to qualify for PSLF forgiveness, perhaps because your residency is in a for-profit hospital, or because you expect to join a for-profit medical group as soon as you begin practice?

Without PSLF on the horizon, paying on your loans during residency or fellowship may not be to your advantage, since it will "capitalize" your loans, and the principal balance will begin to compound. Leaving them on deferral means you'll continue to accrue debt on a "simple interest" basis.

If PSLF is off the table, can you still use IDR to reduce your monthly payments, in order to qualify for the loan forgiveness built into the income-driven plan itself?

> You can still use Income-Driven Repayment to reduce your monthly payments, but...

> Interest will accrue to your loan at a relatively high cost, compared to other forms of borrowing, and this student loan interest will almost certainly not be deductible once you begin earning higher income as an attending.

> Any dollars unpaid after 20 or 25 years may be forgiven, but that forgiveness will be taxable. For example, if you have $100,000 of remaining loan balance forgiven in 2041, you will receive a 1099 at the end of that year showing $100,000 of income you must declare on your taxes, and you will have to pay the resulting tax out-of-pocket.

This chapter has only scratched the surface of the complexity of decisions around your student loans. We hope it has provided enough background to help you begin to explore your best options for getting your own student loan balance to zero, as quickly and efficiently as possible.

Politicians promise to "bend the curve," reducing future medical costs through various "reforms," which often translate down the road into cuts in reimbursement rates. There is another curve you need to bend *upwards*—the curve of compound wealth, carrying you toward financial independence. To do this, you must maximize the after-tax return on every savings dollar.

Chapter 9: Bending the Curve

"A penny saved is a penny earned."

Ben Franklin

Back in our grandparents' day, some number of virtuous people watched every nickel and dime they spent, saved a few precious dollars each week, and then stuffed those savings in the mattress, hid them in a cookie jar or deposited them at the local savings and loan.

This is the "pay yourself last" model of savings. With enough self-discipline, frugality, and foresight, you can follow this strategy and use it to build walkaway wealth.

Good luck with that. Pay yourself last is no longer a realistic strategy for savings. We live in a richer, safer world than our grandparents did, but also a more complex and confusing one, where the demands on our time, attention and financial resources are much greater. Few of us have that simpler world's emotional commitment to thrift. If you plan to save whatever you have left at the end of the month, you are liable to end up out-of-money days before you are out-of-month.

Instead, you should pay yourself *first*. To be most effective, savings should follow what we call MATRIX™ principles. You should always work to:

> - **M**aximize
> - **A**fter-**T**ax
> - **RI**sk-adjusted
> - Return (the key variable, represented by X)

Let's get very specific about how you can best use MATRIX principles to build your wealth, based on a few moving parts—term, interest rate, tax effects, and risk status.

First, recognize that a dollar paid toward reducing the principal on a student loan has the same effect on your net worth as a dollar saved and used to purchase an investment. Deciding whether making investments or paying down debt is more to your advantage simply requires a comparison between the return or interest rate, the tax treatment, and the risk (if any).

Your first priority should *always* be maximizing pre-tax savings to your employer retirement savings plan—usually a 401(k) or 403(b). Those contributions will be withdrawn automatically from your paycheck, and your employer will often match a portion of your savings. This is "free money" in your account.

Let's examine why this type of savings is so much more effective, by looking at the after-tax consequence of directing $10,000 of income toward pre-tax vs. after-tax savings:[12]

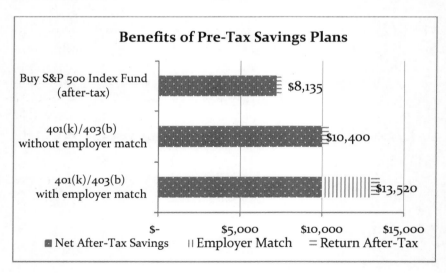

---

[12] We are assuming gross income of $200,000, which suggests a 28% marginal tax bracket for a married couple. We are illustrating pre-tax savings plans both with and without a 50% employer match on the first $6,000 of savings, and assuming investment returns are on the low side at 4% per year. *If tax rates and/or investment returns are higher, the pre-tax option becomes even more attractive.*

As you can see, over the course of a year, the pre-tax savings plan is very hard to beat, especially when it comes with an employer match. The higher your earnings, and the higher your tax bracket, the more significant the advantage of pre-tax savings.

For most of our physician clients, employer-based retirement savings plans have been the foundation of their financial independence, representing the majority of their investment net worth at retirement. Those savings might be in the form of a 403(b) for doctors working for a non-profit hospital system, or of a 401(k) for those working for a for-profit hospital or medical practice. In some cases, those savings plans may be supplemented by a profit-sharing plan for the self-employed, or even (for a lucky few), by an actual pension benefit.

What if you buy into the central thesis of this book, and decide to really push savings? You have already maxed-out on all pre-tax employer savings opportunities, and you want to save additional dollars after-tax. Where should they go?

Again, understand that a dollar of principal paid down against a debt has the same immediate effect on your net worth as a dollar saved to a bank account. *Debt paydown is a form of savings, and sometimes the most effective form.*

With both direct savings and debt paydown on an equal footing, you should direct your after-tax savings dollars using MATRIX™ principles, toward the *maximum after-tax risk-adjusted return.*[13] Consider one set of possible choices:

> ➤ Pay down a non-deductible medical school loan at 6.8%.

---

[13] The tax code gets ever more complex. Depending on income, the tax rate on dividends and long-term capital gains could be as low as 0% and as high as 23.8%. Your mortgage interest might be fully-deductible, or entirely non-deductible. The devil is in the details, and the nature of the tax devil changes frequently and capriciously. Hence the importance of the *principle* of after-tax return, rather than the specific *sequence* offered here.

➤ Pay down your home mortgage, which carries a tax-deductible 3.5% interest rate. (An after-tax cost of 2.5%.)

➤ Buy a bank CD at 1.5%, with no market risk.

➤ Buy a stock index fund in a taxable account, with a projected return of 4% per year, subject to stock market risk.[14] (An implied after-tax return of 3.0%, assuming 23.8% tax rates on dividends and capital gains.)

Here is a visual of this opportunity set:

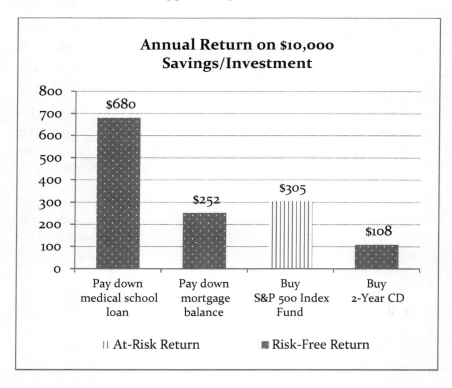

---

[14] We'll discuss how to think more clearly about stock market returns in Chapter 10.

Based on the principle of highest after-tax, risk-adjusted return, the optimal sequence looks like this:

> ➤ The highest return available to you is a risk-free 6.8%, by paying down medical school loans.

> ➤ Once those loans are paid off, the stock fund "pays" a slightly higher after-tax return (about 3%) than the mortgage at 2.5%, but the return on mortgage paydown is risk-free. Paying down mortgage principal is the better risk-adjusted choice.

So 401k first, school loans second, mortgage third and stock fund fourth. The bank certificate, yielding just over 1% after-tax, has poor wealth-building potential, and rarely makes sense for a physician paying high tax rates.

Keep in mind that this sequence is based upon a specific fact-pattern, at a specific point in time, under a specific tax regime. Given different interest rates, financial markets conditions, or tax rates, an entirely different sequence of savings might make more sense. But the principle would be unchanged—*always direct dollars to the highest risk-adjusted after-tax opportunity*.

Let's dive a bit deeper. If the cost of a non-deductible loan is the same as the interest rate on a tax-free municipal bond, you'll get the same balance sheet result—both immediately and in the long-term—from choosing either to repay the loan or buy the bond. So far, so simple.

But what if you could *change* one of those rates? Perhaps you could buy a new tax-free bond with a higher interest rate—*higher* numbers are better for assets. Or you might be able to re-finance the loan at a reduced rate—*lower* numbers are better for loans.

So be alert to opportunities to reduce the effective interest rate on your loans. For example, absent loan forgiveness, it may be to your advantage to refinance your federal student loans at a lower rate through a private lender. If you own a home and have substantial equity, it might be possible to refinance your non-deductible student loans with a tax-deductible home equity loan. Driving down loan costs, or maximizing investment returns, can both be powerful complements to MATRIX™ sequencing.

To demonstrate the potential benefits of MATRIX™ sequencing, consider two scenarios:

1) **A Little Bit of Everything (ALBOE):** This is the typical fact pattern for young doctors, even those who make a commitment to savings from the very beginning of their practices. In this example, we assume total savings of 25% of pre-tax income. Our hypothetical physician couple buys a house and finances with a 15-year mortgage. They prepay the mortgage, double up on their monthly payments toward credit cards, and put any extra savings dollars toward student loans. They begin to make discretionary after-tax investments, starting at $10,000 per year. Once the student loans and mortgage are paid off, they max out their 401ks.

2) **Maximize after-tax risk-adjusted return (MATRIX™):** In this example, we illustrate buying the same house at the same price on the same date, and we end up with the exact same after-tax dollars for consumption. But we make supporting choices using MATRIX™ principles, optimizing the savings/debt paydown sequence so each dollar delivers maximum impact.[15]

The table on the next page shows the moving parts of the two scenarios, while the graph on the following page projects the terminal value of this physician couple's functional net worth at retirement, after thirty years of debt paydown, saving, and investing.

---

[15] This is a simplified analysis. The specific cash flows going to various "buckets" (debt paydown, pre-tax savings, after-tax savings) varies from year to year, but they always follow the optimal MATRIX™ sequence. We control for consumption; each scenario leaves this physician family with exactly the same after-tax dollars to spend.

Comparison of debt-paydown & saving strategies:

Assumptions:	ALBOE	MATRIX
Gross income	$300,000	$300,000
Marginal tax rate (ordinary income)	28%	28%
Tax rate (capital gains & dividends)	23.8%	23.8%
Credit card balances	$20,000	$20,000
Credit card rate	12.99%	12.99%
Student loan balances	$185,000	$185,000
Student loan rate	6.8%	6.8%
Home purchase price	$325,000	$325,000
Down payment	$50,000	$50,000
Mortgage principal	$300,000	$300,000
Mortgage term	15 years	30 years
Mortgage interest rate	3.25%	3.75%
Pre-tax retirement strategy	Capture match	Maximum
Pre-tax retirement savings	$4,500	$36,000
Match	$4,500	$4,500
After-tax investment/year	$10,000	$0
Projected investment return	6%	6%
Taxable income	$285,247	$252,096
Federal taxes paid	$79,869	$705,87
Effective annual savings	$79,131	$88,413
Net dollars for consumption in year one	$141,000	$141,000

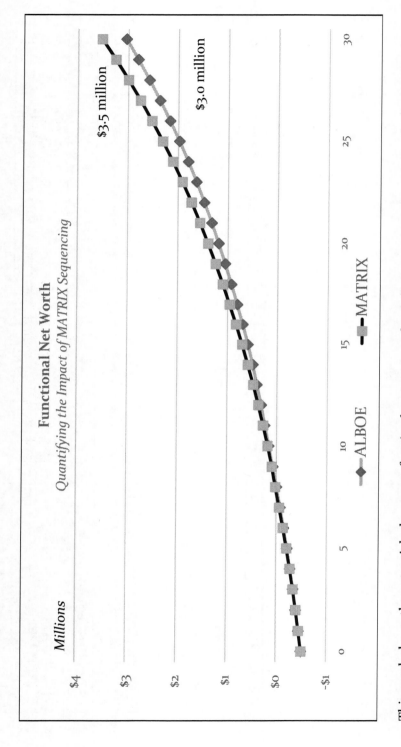

Functional Net Worth
Quantifying the Impact of MATRIX Sequencing

Millions

$4

$3

$2

$1

$0

-$1

$3.5 million

$3.0 million

0   5   10   15   20   25   30

◆ ALBOE   ■ MATRIX

This graph shows the potential advantage of optimal sequencing of cash flows. It represents a projection only, and cannot be guaranteed in any way.

What you observe on the prior page demonstrates a key principle—*following best-practice financial decision-making can have profound, measurable benefits, especially if those best practices are followed from the beginning of your career through its end.*[16]

You have now determined how much savings, as a percentage of income, you intend to put away, and used MATRIX™ principles to determine the optimal sequence of savings. How can you make sure those intended savings actually happen?

Just as with pre-tax retirement plan savings, which come out of your paychecks before you even see them, you should make the other elements of your savings plan automatic and predictable.

Most employers can set up auto-payments to multiple bank accounts. Set up one master savings account, and have your employer direct a fixed percentage of your compensation to it. From this account, make automatic transfers to pay down loans, build cash in a reserve account, fund 529 college savings accounts, or buy investments.

Your objective is to shift enough income from your paycheck to fund all of your savings priorities, before a single dollar flows to the operating account from which you pay your various living expenses. As long as you avoid accumulating any consumer debt, any spending you can fund from the operating account is responsible.

---

[16] We can't emphasize too strongly that MATRIX™ is a *principle* that can be used to construct an optimal sequence at a given point in time. The principle must be applied flexibly and dynamically, and your plan should be updated as underlying conditions change. For example, a large decline in stock prices would raise the expected return on stocks, making an after-tax stock investment more attractive. An increase in interest rates would change mortgage rates, possibly making mortgage paydown more compelling. *Your MATRIX plan is a living document, which should always reflect current economic conditions.*

Understand that Wall Street's promise of superior investment performance rarely comes true for individual investors. Instead of counting on superior investment returns to build wealth, aim for high savings rates.

Chapter 10: Investors Behaving Badly

> *"First, do no harm."*
>
> *Hippocratic Oath*

The Father of Medicine's advice to physicians, back in the 5th century B. C., is also sound counsel for investors today. Better to do nothing than to do something harmful—and the data clearly show that most active investing strategies do harm; they subtract from portfolio returns rather than adding to them.

Here is the data on mutual fund investor performance from research firm DALBAR, for the twenty-year period ending December 31, 2015:[17]

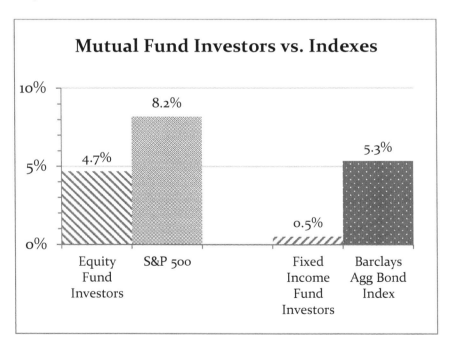

Understand what these data mean—it is not that the typical equity mutual *fund* underperformed the market by 43%. It is that the

---

[17] *DALBAR Quantitative Analysis of Investor Behavior 2016.*

typical *investor* in mutual funds underperformed—by choosing the wrong funds, by being in or out of the market at the wrong times, by chasing performance in up markets and panicking during down markets—in short, by trying to do better than the markets, investors did much worse.

But wait a bit. You are not some Average Joe or Jane off the street. You are a physician, the brightest of the bright. Obviously, you will do better than average, right?

Wrong, almost certainly. Most individuals make decisions about their investments that are remarkably sub-optimal. Research in the emerging discipline of behavioral economics suggests that these poor outcomes are not the result of *cognitive* deficits, nor are they *informational* disadvantages. They are powerful, persistent and intrinsic *behavioral* biases.[18]

In other words, being whip-smart won't save you from being greedy or fearful, nor will it cure you of confirmation bias, framing effects or attribution errors.

The power of behavioral effects on financial decisions shows up at the most basic levels. Among the researchers on behavioral economics are neuroscientists, who can observe on PET or fMRI scans how economically-identical financial decisions can actually be processed in different parts of the brain, depending on how the decisions are framed.

Consider one central insight of behavioral economics: *Most individuals are over-confident about almost everything, almost all the time.* In general, this over-confidence is a survival trait. Who would have asked their future spouse out on a date, cultivated a potato, eaten an oyster, crossed the oceans to the New World, written a first novel, or signed up to take the MCATs, without

---

[18] In fact, some data on identical twins raised in separate households appears to demonstrate that investment success is largely based on innate psychological traits, not on experience or training. In other words, Warren Buffett was born, not made.

healthy self-confidence?

Unfortunately, over-confidence can be deadly for investors, since long-term investment success is based largely on a disciplined understanding of what we can and cannot predict. Yet if there is one essential characteristic of most physicians, it is self-confidence. If you are a surgical specialist, poised above someone's left ventricle with scalpel in hand, you had better not be paralyzed by self-doubt.

That sort of robust confidence simply isn't an asset for an investor. Successful investing requires both a different technical skill set and a different psychological makeup than those that make you effective as a physician.[19]

Besides, even if you think you might possess the right stuff to be a superior investor, it isn't worth your time to find out. A typical doctor works 55 hours or more each week. He already has less free time than most people. Let's assume he has been in practice for five or ten years, and has built up $250,000 in investments. Why not manage that portfolio himself, and save an advisor's fees?

Let's run the numbers. If he spends five hours a week on his investments, that adds up to 250 hours a year. Let's assume his research and active management work out, and he beats the markets, net of fees and costs, by 2% per year. (Not bloody likely, says the data, but let's proceed.)

He has made a profit from his investment skill of $5,000. So for each of his 250 hours of work, he's earned $20—less than a typical waiter takes home after a busy night at TGIFriday's. And this assumes he finds the persistent return advantage most professional investors fail to realize, instead of the large disadvantage experienced by most individual investors.

So keep your strategy as simple and automatic as possible, especially

---

[19] Research suggests that *everyone* is systematically and consistently over-confident...except for those suffering from clinical depression, who are able to assess their own abilities quite accurately. So you might want to be sure your investment advisor has a scrip for Zoloft.

starting out, when you don't have enough capital for superior investment performance to have meaningful impact anyway.

To get richer, faster, you simply need to save more.

In your first years of practice, save your time and energy by adopting a radically simple investment strategy, designed to capture the core returns available in the financial markets.

Chapter 11: A Simple Plan

"Make everything as simple as possible, but not simpler."

Albert Einstein

Now you understand why trying to beat the market is a sub-optimal use of your scarce time and attention as a physician, especially in your early years in practice when you have only limited investment capital. But what is the alternative? Should you just let money pile up in your bank accounts and leave it in a money market fund in your retirement accounts?

Absolutely not. From the beginning of your investing career, you should follow a set of investing principles that will work for the rest of your life:

1) Invest the core of your portfolio in assets with the potential for real growth above inflation. This means common stocks or mutual funds that invest primarily in common stocks. Inevitably, this means most of what you own will fluctuate in value.

2) Diversify.

3) Engage in no investment activity that does not have a documented and measurable advantage. (No day-trading in between patients.)

4) Keep fees and costs low.

5) Think long-term and measure long-term. Ignore the short term. In fact, don't even open your statements if the market is going through a bad patch.

6) Utterly ignore volatility, headlines, CNBC, *The Wall Street Journal, Barron's, Mad Money* with Jim Cramer; as well as any investment advice you receive from your

colleagues, your patients, your golf buddy, or the investment banker in the paceline on your Sunday morning bike ride. (Especially ignore Jim Cramer.)

Let's turn these principles into a sensible, practical, and utterly simple investment strategy:

> ➢ 100% S&P 500 Stock Index Fund

This strategy commits the core of your portfolio to U.S. common stocks, which have delivered superior returns over most long-term periods. Even better, index funds are low-cost, tax-efficient, and by definition will closely track the performance of the broad stock indexes.

That's it. No 200-day moving averages, no Dow Theory buy and sell signals, no market forecasts, no Power Lunches watching Maria Bartiromo, no covered-call writing, no newsletter subscriptions. No noise and nonsense.

This strategy has three key advantages:

1) You will always capture the core returns available in the U.S. equity market, the deepest, most liquid, and best regulated in the world.

2) You will not have to worry about securities selection, timing, or periodic rebalancing. You own one thing—a broad basket of securities—and one thing only, so there is nothing to select, no decision you need to time, and nothing that ever needs rebalancing between asset classes.

3) You will never have to worry about how your portfolio has performed compared to the market, because you own the market. You have eliminated the primary driver of long-term underperformance, which is the doomed attempt to achieve superior *future* performance by examining *past* performance.

Is this an optimal lifetime investment strategy? Not precisely. It does not take full advantage of the economic "free lunch" provided by diversification across a broader selection of assets. If you had $1,000,000 in investment assets, we'd surely suggest a more complex and diversified portfolio.

But you don't yet have $1 million, or anything close. What you have right now is significant debt, an increased income, and a challenging, time-consuming job. With limited investment capital, the marginal advantages of a more-diversified portfolio are unlikely to compensate you for the time you would need to spend monitoring your holdings and making decisions about when to rebalance and which holdings to prioritize.

With this simple strategy, you have every reason to expect that you will earn better long-term returns than most individual investors. In your early years of practice, that is really all you need. *Instead of trying to beat the markets, focus on hitting your savings targets.*

When should you begin thinking about a more diversified, more complicated portfolio? We suggest you wait until you have been in practice for at least three years. This is enough time to have your savings habits firmly in place, and to accumulate enough investment assets in your pre-tax employee savings plans for best-practice investing to begin to have a measurable advantage.

Focusing on your savings rate, instead of some complex investment strategy, also helps to highlight one of the most important and counter-intuitive aspects of wealth accumulation. As a saver, you will be a *net buyer* of investment assets for at least the next two decades. Buyers always, *always* benefit from lower prices, whether they are buying stocks, bonds, commercial real estate, skim milk, or toilet paper.

For savers, bear markets are good news; every bear market is an opportunity to buy quality assets on sale and get rich quicker. Consider the following chart:

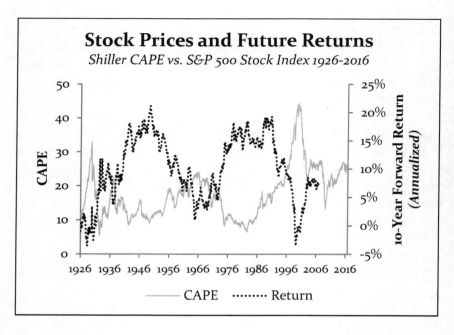

Stock Prices and Future Returns
Shiller CAPE vs. S&P 500 Stock Index 1926-2016

The solid light gray line above represents the price of the stocks in the S&P 500, compared to trailing earnings. The black dotted line represents the average annual return on the S&P for the subsequent ten-year period. The highest value on the gray line was at the peak of the stock market bubble in 1999, when stocks sold for an astonishing 45 times trailing earnings. If we look directly below the 1999 peak, we see a low point on the dotted line, indicating that for the ten years after March of 1999, stocks had an average return of *negative* 3% per year.

This is a compelling visual of a simple truth about investing—*when stock prices are high, future returns will be low, and when stock prices are low, future returns will be high.*[20]

The ideal fact pattern for you as a retirement saver is a stock market

[20] Economist Robert Shiller of Yale University shared the Nobel Prize for Economics in 2014 for his creation of the Shiller CAPE (Cyclically-Adjusted Price-Earnings), which established the systematic relationship between trailing inflation-adjusted earnings and forward stock market returns.

that declines continuously until you retire, and then climbs continuously for the rest of your life. Obviously, neither of these scenarios (constant decline, constant increase) will happen. We just want you to be able to recognize the economic good news implicit in periodic bad news about markets and the economy.

We've been in the investment business since 1978. For most of that period, during the great bull market of 1982 to 2000, the investment winds were at our backs. For almost two decades, stock market returns averaging more than 17% a year piled up wealth as if by magic. Back then, high investment returns could make up for low savings rates.

Since 2000, the investment winds have been in our faces, not at our backs. That doesn't mean you can't build financial independence. But we can't expect investment miracles to make up for savings deficits, and we can't afford to squander any portion of today's modest investment returns through the typical individual investor's reactive, error-prone attempts at active investment management.

The single decision most likely to work against attaining walkaway wealth is buying too much house. Despite the fact that the U.S. housing market crashed the entire world economy in 2008, the illusion persists that residential real estate is a "can't lose" investment proposition.

Chapter 13: The Doctor House

*"Home is that place where, when you have to go
there, they have to take you in."*

Robert Frost, *Death of the Hired Man*

The real estate and mortgage industries have programmed us to
believe that, "Your home is your best investment." Even unusually
intelligent Americans, like physicians, tend to buy into this
proposition. But the data do not support it.

Here are some key facts:

> **Historically, houses have appreciated more slowly
> than equities.** The best data on both asset classes,
> which comes from Nobel Prize-winning economist
> Robert Shiller of Yale University, shows that the real
> (inflation-adjusted) price return on stocks has been
> more than three times higher than for houses. But this
> is only part of the story. [21]

> **Houses have costs, while stocks can produce
> dividends.** Once you buy a house, your expenses have
> just begun. You must pay taxes, utilities, upkeep, and
> insurance. On the other hand, as of mid-year 2016, the
> S&P 500 Stock Index paid a dividend yield of 2.1%, on
> top of potential price increases.

> **Much more than you expect, your house will also
> drive indirect costs.** For example, if every other garage
> on the block contains a Porsche or Mercedes, it can be

---

[21] As mentioned in the last chapter, Yale's Robert Shiller won the Nobel
Prize for his work on the relationship of stock market earnings to
investment return. Working with economist Karl Case of Harvard
University and Wellesley College, he also co-created the Case-Shiller
Housing Price Index, released monthly by Standard & Poor's, which tracks
home prices in 20 metropolitan areas.

uncomfortable driving a used Toyota Camry. Status-signaling expenses like private school tuition, automobiles, even where you vacation, can actually be higher than the direct cost of owning your home.

Here's a visual of Shiller's data:

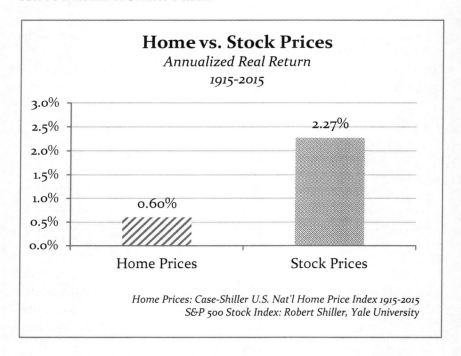

Keep in mind that this reflects only the inflation-adjusted price of homes, and not the fact that houses require maintenance and repair.

For purposes of illustration, let's assume a typical house costs an average of 2% of its value per year to maintain—an amount in the middle of the standard estimate of 1% to 4% per year. What does that suggest about total returns for houses and stocks?

We'll simply add the 2.1% current dividend for the S&P 500 Stock Index to, and deduct the projected 2% upkeep cost of the house from, the historical real price change of each asset.

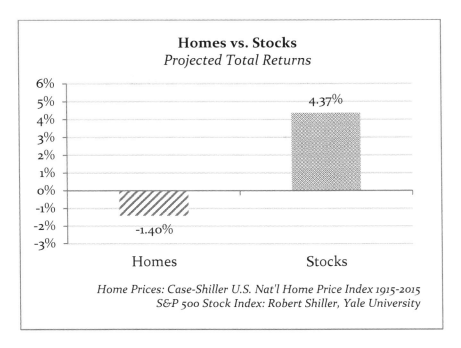

Homes vs. Stocks
Projected Total Returns

Home Prices: Case-Shiller U.S. Nat'l Home Price Index 1915-2015
S&P 500 Stock Index: Robert Shiller, Yale University

The result is an annual net difference of more than 5% per year.

Buy too much house, and you're likely to compound this difference in return and net cost over many years. You can expect the difference in your net worth at retirement to be profound. *Avoiding becoming "house poor" is the single most important lifestyle choice a new physician can make in her first three years of practice.*

With interest rates near historic lows, it can be tempting to pile mortgage debt on top of school loans. Why not take advantage of low-cost money to buy more house?

You may be able to service the 3.5% interest cost of a jumbo mortgage without breaking a sweat, but it will still take a generation to pay off the principal. Not only that, the larger house you buy with the bigger, cheaper mortgage will also come with higher operating expenses. Unlike the monthly fixed-rate mortgage payments, those operating costs will increase with inflation.

Should you rent instead of buy? Probably not. At current interest rates, in most cities in the U.S., it still makes sense to buy instead of renting—*if you plan to stay in your home for five or more years.* (Over shorter periods, the transaction costs are likely to make a house purchase unprofitable.)

For most higher-income earners it is economically better to buy your forever home than to rent it. But that does not mean that buying *any* home, regardless of size or cost, will be a financially superior choice to renting.

If you are renting a two-bedroom apartment, buying a two-bedroom condo is probably a smart decision. But if you move from that same apartment to a "starter home" that is 5,500 square feet and costs $1.5 million—a scenario we've seen more than once with young physicians—there is only the most remote chance that it will pay off in the form of higher net worth at retirement.

A beautiful house in a safe neighborhood can be one of life's great joys. Almost all of our clients own their homes. Just don't make the mistake of believing that your home is likely to be a profitable investment asset. Understand that it is an expense, expect that owning more house will make it harder to accumulate walkaway wealth, and you have positioned yourself to make a more informed and rational house-buying decision.

By making a limited set of positive, conscious and intentional decisions in your first years as an attending physician, you can put yourself on the less-traveled road toward financial independence. We suggest that you focus on seven strategies during your first years of medical practice.

Chapter 13: The Seven Strategies

"Put the big rocks in first."

Chemistry professor to freshman students[22]

No choice, strategy or set of habits can guarantee a specific financial outcome, any more than you can guarantee admission to a specific medical school based on grade point average. But there are best practices that can maximize your chances of getting the results you want.

We've observed the lives and habits of successful physicians over more than thirty years. We have identified seven strategies that can help point you toward financial success.

1) **Understand your actual cash flow.** (It will be less than you think.) As a resident and fellow with earnings around $50,000 per year, taxes took a relatively small bite. But as an attending physician with an income of $200,000 or more per year (for example) your gross income may be four times higher, but the actual cash flow you can spend will *not* be four times greater. Out of $200,000 of gross income, depending on the state in which you practice, you could easily be left with less than $130,000 per year after taxes, malpractice insurance, retirement savings and benefits costs.

2) **Get the basic protections in place first**. You will need life insurance, disability insurance (to the extent it remains available), property/casualty and umbrella liability insurance. Malpractice insurance, of course, if it is not already in place as part of your employment.

---

[22] If you don't recognize this punchline to a very old story, send us an email and we will explain it.

3) **Pay yourself first, and automatically.** For most physicians, this means contributing to a pre-tax retirement savings plan. It could be a 401k through an employer, or a self-employed retirement plan you set up yourself. Maximize pre-tax savings first, for both spouses. The percentage of income that you save will be the primary driver of your growth in net worth. *Only consider after-tax savings if you have already maxed-out your pre-tax retirement plans, and if you already have your insurance protections and your emergency fund in place.*

4) **Begin to build up an emergency cash reserve of three to six months of living expenses.** Even if you never have a financial emergency (as most of us do not), this reserve will have profound value in terms of how you see your finances. By putting dollars aside from each paycheck, instead of spending until your checking account is empty, you are training yourself to live below your means.

5) **Make sure you have a will, and update it to reflect your family situation and new income profile.** In working with your estate attorney, assume you've already accumulated several million dollars, and make the necessary provisions to safeguard and manage it. Hopefully in five or ten years you will have your million. In the midst of a busy career, it will be very easy to put off revising your will. So assume from the beginning that you are going to have meaningful assets, and plan for how to use them to protect those you love.

6) **Buy less house, in a good school district.** The smartest buy is usually an understandable, well-built used house, not a trendy new McMansion. Get pre-qualified for a mortgage. Avoid money pits. To a much greater degree than you expect, the cost of upkeep and utilities will scale with the size and

luxury of your home, and the extent and beauty of your grounds. Finance using a 30-year, fixed-rate mortgage.[23]

7) **Choose your friends wisely.** Remember the concept of social comparison—the more uniform and expensive the lifestyles of your friends, the higher the pressure to comply with the implicit status expectations of your peer group. Some of our most financially successful clients have the most eclectic groups of friends.

---

[23] In other financial guides for doctors, we've seen the advice that you should always finance with a 15-year mortgage. We disagree with this absolute. Sometimes a shorter-term mortgage is good, sometimes bad. If you can finance for 30 years at 4.0% tax-deductible, instead of for 15 years at 3.5%, and use the extra monthly cash flow to pay down a non-deductible 6.8% medical school loan, there is absolutely no question you will be better off. Once the med school loan is paid off, *then* you can aggressively pre-pay the 30-year mortgage. At the end of the day, this sequence will have *all* loans paid off sooner, will minimize your total after-tax interest costs, and will result in significantly higher terminal net worth.

Without much fanfare, a small number of doctors have escaped the status trap. They choose to delay scaling up their lifestyle when they begin practice, and as a result secure a financial advantage that lasts for decades.

Chapter 14: The Staged-In Lifestyle

"Who wants to live like a resident? I'm doing everything I can to forget those years."

Young Physician

Nobody forgets their years as a resident. Long hours, poor pay, life-changing decisions made at the end of a thirty-hour shift. There is no way to get enough hours of clinical experience without pushing the envelope of what even smart, motivated people can survive without breaking down.

So when one of our physician friends told us we were ignoring the most powerful financial independence strategy, which was to continue to live like a resident, we were skeptical. Who would want to do that? He quickly made clear what he was suggesting—*live like a resident for a few more years, while earning as an attending, to get a quick start on financial independence.*

Let's run the numbers. We'll use a hypothetical physician couple, and designate the date when they start practice and begin earning that decent paycheck the beginning of Year One. Here's how they might choose to allocate their increased after-tax income to jump-start their increase in net worth:

The Staged-In Lifestyle

	Year One	Year Two	Year Three
Increased Income	$120,000	$120,000	$120,000
Pre-Tax Savings	($36,000)	($36,000)	($36,000)
Available Income	$84,000	$84,000	$84,000
Home			($10,000)
Cars	($4,000)	($4,000)	($10,000)
Travel	($10,000)	($5,000)	($5,000)
Other	($3,000)	($5,000)	($5,000)
Total Lifestyle	($21,000)	($13,000)	($30,000)
Additional savings	$65,000	$70,000	$50,000

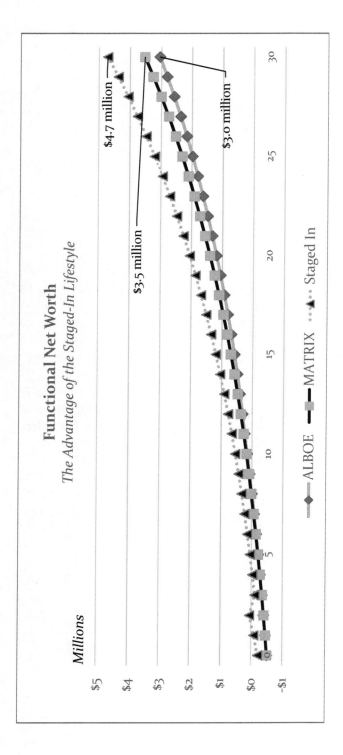

Functional Net Worth
The Advantage of the Staged-In Lifestyle

Millions

$5
$4
$3
$2
$1
$0
-$1

$4.7 million
$3.5 million
$3.0 million

5   10   15   20   25   30

ALBOE   MATRIX   Staged In

Note that in both prior scenarios, *A Little Bit of Everything* and *MATRIX*, the house was bought immediately in Year One of practice, and the initial negative net worth reflects the $300,000 mortgage in addition to $185,000 of student loans. In *The Staged-In Lifestyle*, the same house is purchased at the beginning of Year Four, resulting in a decline in net worth in the amount of the $300,000 mortgage debt assumed at that time.

Over three years, continuing to rent while deferring the gratification of buying a new house and new furniture, and buying one new car instead of two, makes $185,000 additional savings available, enough to retire the typical physician's education loans. (Note that the example assumes that you sign the contract for purchase of a new house, and make a deposit, toward the end of year three.)

What is the long-term effect of easing into the new lifestyle, instead of putting it all in place right away? Take a look at the facing page— *saving an additional $185,000 in the first three years of your career is worth an additional $1.2 million at the end of your career.*

In part, the long-term benefits of The Staged-In Lifestyle are simply another manifestation of the time value of money, demonstrating again the power of compound interest. But it is actually more than that, and the benefits of upgrading your lifestyle more slowly are as much psychological as economic.

By making your most important financial choices consciously and on purpose, rather than simply in response to social cues, you are pushing back against society's status expectations. You are establishing your own metrics by which you will measure your success, rather than adopting those promoted by Madison Avenue.

In doing so, you gain control of both your finances and your head. By making the when of your lifestyle upgrades deliberate instead of reactive, the what can become equally intentional—choosing *when* to buy a new house should give you more conscious control of *how much* new house you buy.

The Staged-In Lifestyle gives you the possibility of being free of student loans in a few years, not over a decade or more. Again and again, we've heard from doctors how profound it is to make that final student loan payment.

Only you can decide if this is the right choice for you. We believe it is an option absolutely worth considering.

We live in the age of the Internet, which has both benefits and consequences. Among the benefits is easy access to a wealth of information on every topic imaginable. Among the negative consequences is an explosion of do-it-yourself activity, even in areas where training and experience have great value.

Chapter 15: The Advisor Advantage

> *"There are two ways to acquire wisdom. You can buy it, or you can rent it."*
>
> Benjamin Franklin

What doctor has not had a conversation with a patient who suggests an alternative diagnosis or treatment based on something he read on WebMD?

Just like the patients surfing WebMD on their iPads, you may well be inclined to act as your own financial advisor, using online resources to help you to make financial decisions and manage your portfolio.

We think this is usually a bad idea, for several reasons.

First, the urge to do-it-yourself violates one of the primary drivers of human intellectual and material progress—the principle of comparative advantage. The entire world gets richer when we each do what we are best at, and let others do what they do best.

Second, doing it yourself ignores one of the fundamental realities of life for physicians—their lack of time.

Third, and most important, doing it yourself requires you to make all of your own mistakes. As financial advisors who entered the business in 1978, and who have observed the financial decisions of hundreds of families over more than thirty-five years, we know exactly how costly it can be to learn-by-doing.

To use an analogy to medical care, what you pay an advisor for is a combination of technical expertise, knowledge of best practices, and clinical experience. Even if you spent all your spare time reading financial planning texts, you would never be able to duplicate the perspective that an experienced financial advisor can provide, based on countless observations of real world economic decision-making by real people.

This kind of hard-earned wisdom about human behavior is one of the principal benefits of having an advisor. You don't have to learn by trial and error, and you don't have to waste your scarce headspace getting up-to-speed on investing, insurance and the other technical aspects of personal finance in the 21st century. That time and attention is better spent keeping current with the advancing state of the medical art.

As a doctor starting practice, you need an advisor to perform six key functions:

1) **Get protection.** Make sure you have put in place the necessary structures and protections for you and your family in the relatively unlikely event of death or disability.

2) **Set goals.** Work with you to set realistic long-term goals, using best-practice financial modeling, and making realistic assumptions about future market returns.

3) **Avoid mistakes.** Be your trusted partner in making the financial decisions needed to build walkaway wealth, especially by helping you to avoid the unforced economic errors that can be so costly to doctors early in their careers.

4) **Invest effectively.** Manage your investments to successfully capture the economic returns available in the financial markets.

5) **Keep score.** Help you keep track of your progress, using metrics that distinguish between financial signal and market noise.

6) **Provide accountability.** Make sure your actual financial behavior matches your intentions, by tracking your net savings and capital accumulation against the targets established in your plan. (Given

the grim statistics on wealth accumulation for most physicians, this may be the most important function of all.)

Notice what is not on this list. You don't need an advisor to beat the markets (few do), to protect you from portfolio declines (a hopeless task and in practice a sales pitch for high-commission insurance policies), or to help you discover the meaning of life.

You need someone who is intelligent, sensible, credentialed and experienced, who will help you to put a solid structure in place, upon which you can build your financial security over decades. *You need to get on track early.*

We discussed earlier why insurance agents are often the first advisors to approach young doctors. The high commissions on whole life insurance provide an attractive payday for an insurance agent. What often results is a physician with good disability insurance coverage, a $10,000 per year premium for a whole life insurance policy she eventually realizes she does not need, and a lasting skepticism about financial advisors.

What doesn't happen is a systematic approach to the payment of debts, setup of savings plans, purchase of a house, and establishment of a network of advisors.

You absolutely need the proper sorts of insurance, especially if you are married, even more so if you have children. But your principal advisor should not earn much of his compensation from commissions on insurance sales—or sales of any other financial product or service, for that matter. The potential for conflict of interest is simply too great.

Until recently, there was no fee-based compensation model designed to deliver competent and objective advice to the group of physicians who need it the most—young doctors starting practice. We believe that is changing, and we hope to help that process along. This book is part of our solution.

In a world where doctors struggle with rational pessimism about the future of the profession, we hope we have offered some reasons for rational long-term optimism about your own personal finances. We wish you a happy, productive and prosperous future. *To your wealth.*

Afterword

In this little book, we've tried to clarify some of the key moving parts of the transition from poorly paid residency or fellowship to well paid practice as an attending physician.

We hope we've helped you to understand how the specific choices you make in your first years in practice—as you are moving, buying a house, furniture and cars, signing up for your employer savings plan, and assembling your team of advisors—can help put you on track toward walkaway financial independence by normal retirement age.

➢ If you have any suggestions about how this guide could be expanded or improved, please email us at triage-md@tgsfin.com.

➢ For more information about *TriageMD*, our fee-based advisory programs for physicians, email us or go to the *TriageMD* website at www.triage-md.com.

➢ If you would like to schedule an initial consultation with one of our financial advisors, please call (800) 525-4075 or email us at triage-md@tgsfin.com.

Since the founding of TGS Financial Advisors in 1990, helping physicians achieve better financial outcomes has been a key focus of our independent advisory practice. If you wish to explore how we can help you make optimal financial decisions today, so you will have more attractive options twenty years from now, we would welcome the opportunity to speak with you.

David A. Burd, CFP®

A graduate of Swarthmore College, David has worked in the investment field since 1978. He co-founded TGS Financial Advisors with Jim Hemphill in 1990.

David's practice concentrates on the financial needs of physicians and medical specialists. He particularly enjoys his work with dual-physician households and multi-generational physician families.

David is married to Charlene, who has a Master's in Education and recently retired from her position as a counselor at Delran Middle School in New Jersey. They have two children, Zachary and Samantha. They live in Voorhees, New Jersey.

James S. Hemphill, CFP®, CIMA®, CPWA®

Jim graduated from Swarthmore College. He began work with his first physician client in 1979. He co-founded TGS Financial Advisors with David Burd in 1990.

Jim creates the content for the firm's TriageMD programs (triage-md.com), a systematic approach to wealth management for physicians. He has presented workshops in hospitals, medical schools, and dental schools.

Jim is married to Amy, who received her Master of Public Health in Epidemiology from Johns Hopkins University in 1998. She works for The Nemours Foundation in Wilmington, Delaware, analyzing medical data sets to improve clinical outcomes. They have two sons, Jack and Alex, and a daughter, Katharine. They live in West Chester, Pennsylvania.

Made in the USA
Lexington, KY
06 February 2019